MEASURE IT!

AUG 2016

Measuring Weight

By T. H. Baer

D1379442

Gareth Stevens
PUBLISHING

Please visit our website, www.garethstevens.com. For a free color catalog of all our high-quality books, call toll free 1-800-542-2595 or fax 1-877-542-2596.

Cataloging-in-Publication Data

Names: Baer, T.H.
Title: Measuring weight / T. H. Baer.
Description: New York : Gareth Stevens Publishing, 2016. | Series: Measure it! | Includes index.
Identifiers: ISBN 9781482438765 (pbk.) | ISBN 9781482438772 (6 pack) | ISBN 9781482438789 (library bound)
Subjects: LCSH: Weight (Physics)–Measurement–Juvenile literature.
Classification: LCC QC106.B34 2016 | DDC 530.8–dc23

Published in 2016 by
Gareth Stevens Publishing
111 East 14th Street, Suite 349
New York, NY 10003

Designer: Laura Bowen
Editor: Ryan Nagelhout

Photo credits: Cover, p. 1 Christopher Futcher/E+/Getty Images; pp. 2–24 (background texture) style_TTT/Shutterstock.com; p. 5 Kzenon/Shutterstock.com; p. 7 (rocks) Todd Kreykes/Shutterstock.com; p. 7 (feathers) Essential Image Media/ Shutterstock.com; p. 9 (bread) nito/Shutterstock.com; p. 11 (ounces) Steve Debenport/ E+/Getty Images; p. 11 (pounds) Sedlacek/Shutterstock.com; pp. 13, 15, 19 (scale) Olga Popova/Shutterstock.com; p. 13 (cat) Africa Studio/Shutterstock.com; p. 15 (pineapple) Jiri Miklo/Shutterstock.com; p. 17 (paper clip) Malll Themd/ Shutterstock.com; p. 19 (dog) Erik Lam/Shutterstock.com; p. 21 Martinvl/ Wikimedia Commons.

Printed in the United States of America

CPSIA compliance information: Batch #CW16GS: For further information contact Gareth Stevens, New York, New York at 1-800-542-2595.

Contents

Boldface words appear in the glossary.

Heavy or Light?

Is your **backpack** heavy? Is your pencil light? How much does each weigh? You can tell they weigh different amounts. There are many different **units** used to measure weight. Let's learn how to use them!

5

Mass Matters

A bucket of feathers weighs less than a bucket of rocks. This is because rocks have more mass. Mass is the amount of matter packed into an area. The more mass packed into an object, the heavier the object is.

more mass

less mass

Ounces and Pounds

There are different systems of measurement. In the US customary system, one of the smallest units used to measure weight is the ounce (oz). Ounces can be grouped together to make bigger measurements. There are 16 ounces in a pound (lb).

1 oz

=

1 pound

16 ounces = 1 pound

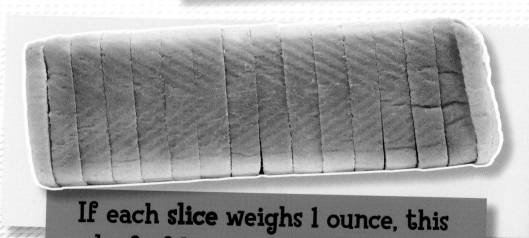

If each slice weighs 1 ounce, this loaf of bread weighs 1 pound.

9

Measuring Tools

We use **scales** to measure weight. Scales measure weight using different units depending on what kind of matter they're weighing. Scales used to measure people often use pounds. Smaller scales used to measure food often use ounces.

weighing
ounces

weighing
pounds

Measure That Cat!

Let's use our measuring units to find out how much this cat weighs. Our scale has lines that mark every 2 pounds and a needle that points to the measurement. When the cat is put on the scale, the needle points halfway between 6 and 8 pounds. That means the cat weighs 7 pounds!

7 pounds

Fruit Weight

We can use pounds and ounces together to measure weight. The scale says this pineapple weighs 26 ounces. How many pounds does it weigh? Since we know there are 16 ounces in a pound, we can subtract that from the weight. The pineapple weighs 1 pound, 10 ounces!

26 oz - 16 oz (1 lb)

=

10 oz

1 lb, 10 oz

Metric Weights

Other countries use the metric system. The milligram (mg) is the smallest unit used to measure weight in the metric system. There are 1,000 milligrams in a gram (g). One paper clip weighs about a gram. There are 1,000 grams in a kilogram (kg).

metric measurements		US measurements
28 grams	=	1 oz
454 grams (or .454 kg)	=	1 lb (or 16 oz)

1 gram	=	1,000 milligrams
1 kilogram	=	1,000 grams

= 1 gram

Measuring in Metric

Let's use metric units to measure the weight of this dog. The scale uses kilograms to measure weight and shows marks for every 5 kilograms. The scale's needle points halfway between 10 and 20 kilograms. This means the dog weighs 15 kilograms!

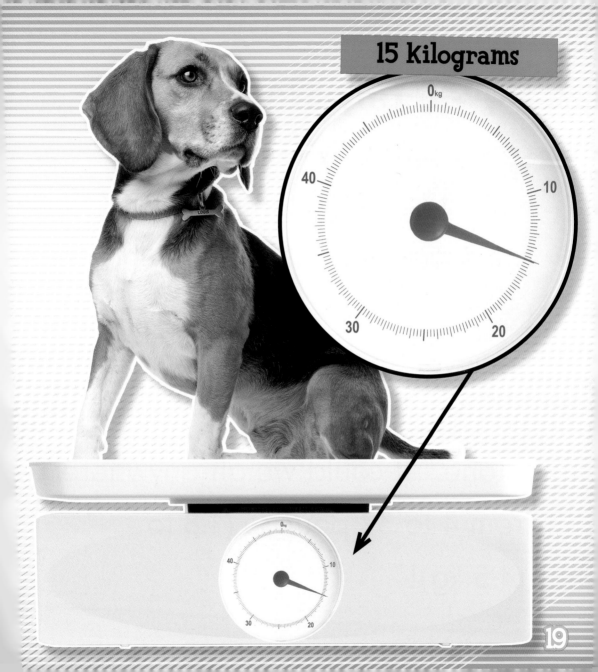

15 kilograms

How Many Stones?

One weird way to measure weight is using stones, which are usually equal to 14 pounds (6.35 kg) today. In the past, however, many towns would pick a rock to use as their own "stone." It could weigh anywhere from 4 to 32 pounds (1.8 to 14.5 kg)!

This weighing stone was used to measure weight in ancient Rome.

Glossary

ancient: relating to a period of time long ago

backpack: a pack carried on the back

scale: a measuring tool that measures using different amounts

slice: a thin, flat piece cut from something

unit: a standard amount used for measuring

For More Information

Books

First, Rachel. *Weigh It! Fun with Weight.* Minneapolis, MN: ABDO Publishing, 2016.

Gardner, Robert. *How Heavy Is Heavy? Science Projects with Weight.* Berkeley Heights, NJ: Enslow Elementary, 2015.

Reinke, Beth Bence. *Measuring Weight.* Ann Arbor, MI: Cherry Lake Publishing, 2014.

Websites

Kids Math
ducksters.com/kidsmath/units_of_measurement_glossary.php
Find out more about different units of measurement on this site.

Measurement Game for Kids
sciencekids.co.nz/gamesactivities/math/measurements.html
Learn more about measuring weight with these fun games.

Unit Weights
numbernut.com/prealgebra/units-mass.php
Find more conversions for different measurements here.

Index